Table of Contents

DC with a Twist Scarf

Designed by Tanis Galik

This elegant yet easy-to-crochet scarf consists of one row of single crochet and one row of double crochet with a twist. It creates a lovely pattern that appears much more difficult than it really is. Make it in a comfy yarn such as Red Heart Soft Yarn for everyday use, or chose a shiny, novelty yarn for evening wear. Either way, it's the perfect scarf for any occasion!

MATERIALS LIST

YARN

Red Heart Soft Yarn (100% acrylic; 256yds/234m per 5oz/140g ball) in color #9522 Leaf

HOOKS AND NOTIONS

Size US J/10 (6mm) crochet hook, or size needed to obtain gauge
Yarn needle

GAUGE

16 dc = 4"(10cm)

FINISHED MEASUREMENTS

6" wide x 64" long (15cm x `73cm)

Special Abbreviations

DCT (double crochet with a twist): Yo, insert hook from front to back in skipped sc (before 3 dc), yo, pull through and across 3 dc, [yo, pull through 2 loops on hook] twice.

Crocheting the Scarf

Chain 255 loosely.

Row 1: Working in back loop only, sc in 2nd ch from hook and in each ch across (254 sc).

(Be careful not to twist the base chain while working.)

Note: By working in the back loop, a 2-loop chain edge is left on the other side. This will match the completed edge along the opposite side of the scarf. No extra edging is necessary.

Row 2: Ch 3 (counts as first dc), skip first sc, *skip next sc, dc in next 3 sc, DCT; rep from * across to last sc, dc in last sc, turn.

Row 3: Ch 1, sc in each dc across, turn.

Repeat Rows 2 and 3 until piece measures 6" (15cm). Fasten off.

Finishing
Weave in ends.

Cowl-Shawl

Designed by Anastasia Popova

Stay warm and fashionable while wearing this beautiful cowl with a shawl collar. It is worked from edge to edge with the star stitch for the cowl and linked stitches (double and treble crochet) for the shawl collar.

MATERIALS LIST

YARN

270 yds worsted weight yarn
Sample shown in Patons Angora
Bamboo (55% bamboo, 35% wool,
10% angora; 80 yds/73 m per
1.75oz/50 g ball), in color #90310
Echinacea, 4 balls

HOOKS AND NOTIONS

Size US H/8 (5mm) crochet
hook, or size needed to obtain
gauge
Four 3/4" buttons
Stitch marker
Yarn needle

Gauge
20 sts and 11 rows = 4.75"/12cm

FINISHED MEASUREMENTS

8.5" wide x 29" long
(21cm x 73cm)

Special Abbreviations

Star Stitch (star st): Insert hook under ch 1 just made, yo and draw up loop, insert hook into side of hdc just made, yo and draw up loop, insert hook into same sp, yo and draw up loop, [insert hook in next st, yo and draw up loop] twice, yo and pull through all loops on hook; ch 1.

Beg star st: Yo, insert hook into 2nd ch from hook, yo and draw up loop, insert hook into same sp, yo and draw up loop, [insert hook in next st, yo and draw up loop] twice, yo and pull through all loops on hook; ch 1.

Linked double crochet (ldc): Insert hook in horizontal bar of last st made, yo and draw up loop, insert hook into next st, yo and pull up loop (3 loops on hook), [yo and pull through 2 loops] twice.

Beg linked double crochet: Insert hook in 2nd ch from hook, yo and draw up loop, insert hook in next st, yo and draw up loop (3 loops on hook), [yo and pull through 2 loops] twice.

Linked treble crochet (ltr): Insert hook in first horizontal bar of last st made, yo and draw up loop, insert hook in 2nd horizontal bar of last st made, yo and draw up loop, insert hook into next st, yo and draw up loop (4 loops on hook), [yo and pull through 2 loops] 3 times.

Beg linked treble crochet: Insert hook in 2nd ch from hook, yo and draw up loop, insert hook in 3rd ch from hook, yo and draw up loop, insert hook in next st, yo and draw up loop (4 loops on hook), [yo and pull through 2 loops] 3 times.

Ldc/tr: Yo, insert hook in horizontal bar of last st made, yo and draw up loop, insert hook into next st, yo and draw up loop (4 loops on hook), [yo and pull through 2 loops] 3 times.

Ltr/dc: Insert hook in first horizontal bar of last st made, yo and draw up loop, insert hook in 2nd horizontal bar of last st made, yo and draw up loop, insert hook into next st, yo and draw up loop (4 loops on hook), yo and pull through 2 loops, yo and pull through 3 loops.

Crocheting the Scarf

Beginning Section
Row 1: Ch 22, ldc in 4th ch from hook (skipped ch-3 counts as ldc) and each ch across, turn (20 ldc).
Row 2 (buttonhole row): Ch 2 (counts as dc unless otherwise specified), ldc in next st, [ch 1, skip next st, dc in next st, ldc in next 3 sts] 3 times, ch 1, skip next st, dc in next st, turn (20 sts).
Row 3: Ch 2, hdc in same st, hdc in each st across, turn (21 sts).
Row 4: Ch 2, star st in each st across to last st, hdc in last st, turn (12 sts).
Row 5: Ch 2, 2 hdc in each ch-1 sp across to last st, hdc in last st, turn (22 sts).
Repeat rows 4-5 three more times.

Increase Section
Row 1: Ch 2, star st in each st across to last st, (hdc, dc) in last st, turn (13 sts).
Row 2: Ch 2, ldc in same sp, hdc in hdc, 2 hdc in each ch-1 sp across to last st, hdc in last st, turn (24 sts).
Row 3: Ch 2, star st in each st across to marker, hdc in hdc (pm), 2 ldc in next st, ldc in last st, turn (15 sts).
Row 4: Ch 2, ldc in same sp, ldc in each st to marker, hdc in hdc (pm), 2 hdc in each ch-1 sp across to last st, hdc in last st, turn (26 sts).
Row 5: Ch 2, star st in each st across to marker, hdc in hdc (pm), ldc in each st to last 2 sts, 2 ldc in next st, ldc in last st, turn (17 sts).
Row 6: Repeat row 4 (28 sts).
Row 7: Repeat row 5 (19 sts).
Row 8: Ch 3, ltr in same sp, ltr in each st to 5 sts before marker, ltr/dc in next st, ldc in next 4 sts, hdc in hdc (pm), 2 hdc in each ch-1 sp across to last st, hdc in last st, turn (30 sts).
Row 9: Ch 2, star st in each st across to marker, hdc in hdc (pm), ldc in next 4 sts, ldc/tr in next st, ltr in each st to last 2 sts, 2 ltr in next st, ltr in last st, turn (21 sts).
Repeat rows 8-9 three more times (27 sts).

Straight Section
Row 1: Ch 3, ltr in each st to 5 sts before marker, ltr/dc in next st, ldc in next 4 sts, hdc in hdc (pm), 2 hdc in each ch-1 sp across to last st, hdc in last st, turn (36 sts).

Row 2: Ch 2, star st in each st across to marker, hdc in hdc (pm), ldc in next 4 sts, ldc/tr in next st, ltr in each st across, turn (27 sts).

Repeat rows 1-2 nine more times, then Row 1 once.

Decrease Section
Row 1: Ch 2, star st in each st across to marker, hdc in hdc (pm), ldc in next 4 sts, ldc/tr in next st, ltr in each st to last 2 sts, skip next st, ltr in last st, turn (26 sts).
Row 2: Ch 3, ltr in next st, skip next st, ltr in each st to 5 sts before marker, ltr/dc in next st, ldc in next 4 sts, hdc in hdc (pm), 2 hdc in each ch-1 sp across to last st, hdc in last st, turn (34 sts).

Repeat rows 1-2 three more times (29 sts).

Row 9: Ch 2, star st in each st across to marker, hdc in hdc (pm), ldc in each st to last 2 sts, skip next st, ldc in last st, turn (18 sts).
Row 10: Ch 2, ldc in next st, skip next st, ldc in each st to marker, hdc in hdc (pm), 2 hdc in each ch-1 sp across to last st, hdc in last st, turn (27 sts).

Repeat Rows 9-10 one more time, then Row 9 once (14 sts).

Row 14: Ch 2, skip next st, hdc in hdc, 2 hdc in each ch-1 sp across to last st, hdc in last st, turn (23 sts).

End Section
Row 1: Ch 2, star st in each st across to last st, hdc in last st (12 sts).
Row 2: Ch 2, 2 hdc in each ch-1 sp across to last st, hdc in last st, turn (22 sts).
Repeat Rows 1-2 three more times.
Row 9: Ch 2, ldc in next st, skip next st, ldc in each st across to last 2 sts, skip next st (20 sts).
Row 10: Ch 2, ldc in each st across. Fasten off.

Finishing
Weave in ends.

Rustically Elegant Shoulder Warmer

Designed by Denise Lavoie

Accessories that keep shoulders warm are usually quick, practical, and fashionable projects just like this one. Take uncomplicated construction, add a saturated jewel-tone yarn, choose a favorite size, and you've got the recipe for a go-to piece that will keep you warm and trendy as you transition through the seasons.

MATERIALS LIST

YARN

1500 (1720, 1940) yds sport weight yarn, held double throughout

Sample shown in Patons Lace Sequins (68% acrylic, 14% polyester, 9% mohair, 9% wool; 344yds/314m per 2.5 oz/70g ball) in color #37201 Aquamarine, 5 (5, 6) balls, held double throughout project

HOOKS AND NOTIONS

Size US J/10 (6mm) and K/10.5 (6.5mm) crochet hook, or size needed to obtain gauge

Yarn needle

Four (4) 5/8" shank buttons

GAUGE

12 sc and 8 rows = 4"(10cm) with smaller hook and yarn held double

FINISHED MEASUREMENTS

20" wide x 24(28,31)" circumference/ 51cm x 61(71, 79)cm

Special Abbreviations

FPdc (front post double crochet): Yo, insert hook from front to back to front around post of indicated st. Yo, pull up a loop. Continue the same as a regular double crochet.

Note: The main body of the shoulder warmer is one long rectangle, with the short edge seamed to one of the longer edges. Stitches are then picked up around the neck opening after seaming and worked back and forth.

Crocheting the Shoulder Warmer

With smaller hook and yarn held double, ch 60.

Row 1: Sc in second ch from hook, and in each ch across (59 sc). Turn.

Row 2: Ch 3 (counts as first dc), dc in next 3 sc, ch 1, sk next 3 sc, (sc, dc, ch 1, dc, sc) in next sc, ch 1, sk next 3 sc, *dc in next 4 sc, ch 1, sk next 3 sc, (sc, dc, ch 1, dc, sc) in next sc, ch 1, sk next 3 sc, rep from * across row, ending with dc in last 4 sc (5 pattern repeats). Turn.

Row 3: Ch 3 (counts as first dc), FPdc in next 3 dc, ch 1, sk next 3 dc, (sc, dc, ch 1, dc, sc) in next dc, ch 1, sk next 3 dc, *FPdc in next 4 dc, ch 1, sk next 3 dc, (sc, dc, ch 1, dc, sc) in next dc, ch 1, sk next 3 dc, rep from * across row, ending with FPdc in last 3 dc, FPdc around ch 3 (5 pattern repeats). Turn.

Repeat Row 3 until piece measures 43 (47, 50)"/ 109 (119, 127)cm from beginning.

Next Row: Ch 1 (counts as first sc), sc in next 3 dc, sc in next ch-1 space, sc in next sc, ch 1, sk next dc, sl st in next ch-1 space, ch 1, sk next dc, sc in next sc, sc in next ch-1 sp, * sc in next 4 dc, sc in next ch-1 space, sc in next sc, ch 1, sk next dc, sl st in next ch-1 space, ch 1, sk next dc, sc in next sc, sc in next ch-1 sp, rep from * across row, ending with sc in final 4 dc. Turn.

Final Row: Ch 1 (counts as first sc), sc in every stitch and ch 1 space across row. Fasten off.

Finishing
Weave in ends. Block to size, stretching to make larger sizes.

Line up A corners and B corner with B point on long edge according to schematic. Sew seam.

Collar
With RS facing and larger hook, attach yarn, still held double, with sl st just to the right of top of seam at neck. Work 81 (92, 103) sc evenly around neck edge, keeping a 1"/2.5cm gap between beginning sc and ending sc. Turn.

Work Rows 2 and 3 of body patt across next two rows. Continue in patt for 10 more rows – 12 rows in all. Work final 2 rows as for main body, ending on the left side of the collar. Do not fasten off.

Left Collar Edge
Work 2 sc in corner. Turn collar 90 degrees clockwise, so that left edge of collar is your working edge. Work 22 sc evenly down side of collar, ending with a final sc into the neck edge (the 1"/2.5cm space left between the 2 sides of collar). Turn.

Work 2 more rows of sc, ending at neck edge. Fasten off.

Right Collar Edge (buttonhole edge)
With larger hook and yarn held double, attach yarn with sl st at top of right side of collar. Work 22 sc down side of collar, ending with a final sc into neck edge. Turn.

Buttonhole Row
Sc into first 4 sc, *ch 1, sk next sc, sc into next 4 sc, rep from * twice more, ending with ch 1, sk next sc, sc into final three sc (4 buttonholes made).

Work a final row of sc, ending at neck edge. Fasten off. Weave in ends.

Sew buttons to inside edge of left side of collar, corresponding to buttonhole placement. Button collar and fold over so several buttons appear on right side of shoulder warmer.

Fair Isle Cowl

Designed by Anastasia Popova

Fair Isle is not just for knitting anymore! Accessorize the whole family with this beautiful versatile cowl/neck warmer. Better yet, combine it with the Fair Isle Hat (from "Quick and Simple Crochet Hats") to wear as a stunning set. The main stitch used in this set is the shallow half double crochet that creates a drapy, squishy pattern unusual for crochet fabric.

MATERIALS LIST

YARN

Worsted weight yarn in three solid colors, one skein of each

Samples shown in Caron Simply Soft (100% acrylic; 315yds/288m per 6oz/170g ball) in colors #9608 Blue Mint (MC) 1 skein, #9754 Persimmon (CC1) 1 skein, #9742 Grey Heather (CC2) 1 skein

HOOKS AND NOTIONS

Size US G/6 (4.25mm) crochet hook

Size US H/8 (5mm) crochet hook, or size needed to obtain gauge

Stitch marker

Yarn needle

GAUGE

17 sts and 12 rows = 4" (10 cm) in shallow hdc using larger hook

FINISHED MEASUREMENTS

21.25" /54 cm circumference

Special Abbreviations

FPdc (front post double crochet): Yo, insert hook from front to back to front around post of indicated st. Yo, pull up a loop. Continue the same as a regular double crochet.

BPdc (back post double crochet): Yo, insert hook from back to front to back around post of indicated st. Yo, pull up a loop. Continue the same as a regular double crochet.

Fdc (foundation double crochet): A technique used to make the foundation chain and first row of dc at the same time.

Beginning fdc: Ch 3, yo, insert hook in 3rd ch from hook, yo and draw up loop, yo and pull through 1 loop (ch made), [yo and pull through 2 loops] 2 times (dc made).

Next and all other fdc: Yo, insert hook under 2 loops of ch at the bottom of st just made, yo and draw up loop, yo and pull through 1 loop (ch made), [yo and pull through 2 loops] 2 times (dc made).

Shdc (shallow half double crochet): Yo, insert hook in horizontal bar behind front and back loops (it helps to tilt the edge towards you) of specified stitch, yo and pull up loop, yo and draw through all loops on hook.

Sdc (shalow double crochet): Yo, insert hook in horizontal bar behind front and back loops (it helps to tilt the edge towards you) of specified stitch, yo and draw up loop, [yo and pull through 2 loops on hook] twice.

Crocheting the Cowl

Rnd 1: With smaller hook and MC, fdc 90. Being careful not to twist, sl st in 1st fdc to join.
Rnds 2-3: Ch 2 (counts as BPdc), BPdc in next st, FPdc in next 3 sts, [BPdc in next 2 sts, FPdc in next 3 sts] around, sl st to join on top of ch 2 (90 sts).

For the next 15 rnds follow Fair Isle chart, while working rnds below:

Rnd 4: With larger hook, ch 1, hdc in each st around.
Rnds 5-18: Shdc in each st around.
Rnd 19: With smaller hook and MC, ch 2 (count as dc), sdc in each st around, sl st in top of ch 2.
Rnds 20-21: Repeat rnds 2-3. Fasten off.

Finishing
Weave in ends.

MC
CC1
CC2

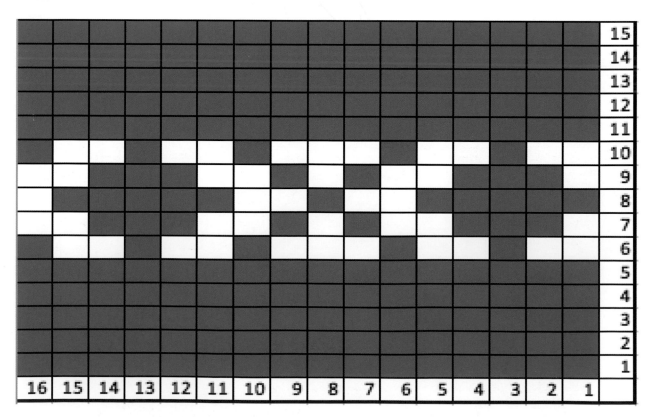

Moc Croc Skinny Cowl

Designed by Melissa Armstrong

The crocodile stitch is one of my favorites, but I find it difficult to teach others - there are many steps to follow, and charts showing overlapping stitches are confusing to new crochet students. I devised this two-part technique after months of experimentation. Be sure to match this cowl with the Moc Croc Hat (from "Quick and Simple Crochet Hats") for an adorable set.

MATERIALS LIST

Yarn

Lion Brand Jiffy (100% acrylic; 135yd/123m per 3oz/85g ball) in color #9866716 Violet, 2 balls

Hooks and Notions

Size US H/8 (5mm) crochet hook, or size needed to obtain gauge

Gauge

Gauge is not critical for this project

Finished Measurements

3" wide x 32" circumference (8cm x 81 cm)

Special Abbreviations

V-St: 2 dc in one sc.

Crocodile Stitch: (5 dc, ch 1, 5 dc) in V-st.

Crocheting the Cowl

First row: Ch 10. Dc in 4th ch from hook (first v-st made). *Skip 2 sts, ch 2, 2 dc in next ch,* rep from * (3 V-sts).

Row 2: Turn. Ch 3, dc in center of V-st, below, *skip 2 sts, ch 2, 2 dc in next V-st,* rep from * once more.

Repeat Row 2 thirty more times.

Crocodile Scales: Turn work sideways.

Row 1: Ch 3, 4 dc into side of V-st, ch 1, 5 dc in opposite side of V-st, skip next V-st, 5 dc in side of last V-st, ch 1, 5 dc in opposite side of V-st (2 Crocodile scales made).

Row 2: Working into back of dc just worked, ch 1, sc into bottom of dc, skip 1, sc in bottom of dc, skip 1, sc into bottom of dc, ch 2, skip first V-st, 5 dc in side of next v-st, ch 1, 5 dc in opposite side of V-st, ch 2 (1 Crocodile Scale made).

Row 3: 5 dc in side of next V-st, ch 1, 5 dc in opposite side of v-st, skip next V-st, 5 dc in side of last V-st, ch 1, 5 dc in opposite side of V-st (2 Crocodile Scales made).

Repeat Rows 2 and 3 thirty more times, ending with Row 2. Fasten off.

Finishing

Cut yarn, leaving an 8"/20cm tail. Sew short ends together. Weave in ends.

Simple Ruffles

Designed by Anastasia Popova

It's got what girls crave - ruffles! Wrap it around your neck, fasten the ends with a knot or a pin, or just let them float. This triangular shawlette is worked from the center top to the bottom points with increases in the middle spine and sides. The main part of the shawl is worked in rows of double crochet with randomly placed rows of "holes," and finished with a border of ruffles.

MATERIALS LIST

Yarn

400 yds sport weight yarn
Sample shown in Lion Brand Vanna's Glamour (96% acrylic, 4% polyester; 202yds/185m per 1.75oz/50g ball) in color #149 Moonstone; 2 balls

Hooks and Notions

Size US F/5 (3.75 mm) crochet hook, or size needed to obtain gauge
Stitch marker
Yarn needle

Gauge

18 dc and 10 rows = 4" (10cm)

Finished Measurements

42" wide x 19" long / 107cm x 48cm

Crocheting the Shawlette

Ch 4.

Row 1: 6 dc in 2nd ch from hook, turn (7 sts).

Row 2: Ch 3 (counts as dc), 2 dc in same st, dc in next 2 sts, 5 dc in next st (pm in 3rd dc made), dc in next 2 sts, 3 dc in last st, turn (15 dc).

Row 3 (solid row): Ch 3, 2 dc in same st, dc in each st to marker, 5 dc in marked st (pm in 3rd dc made), dc in each st to last st, 3 dc in last st, turn (23 sts).

Row 4 (mesh row): Ch 3, dc in same st, ch 1, [dc in next st, ch 1, skip next st] to marker, (dc, ch 1, dc, ch 1, dc) in marked st (pm in middle dc), *[ch 1, skip next st, dc in next

st], rep from * to last st, ch 1, 2 dc in last st, turn (31 sts).

Repeat [solid row 3 times, mesh row 1 time, solid row 2 times, mesh row 1 time, solid row 4 times, mesh row 1 time] 2 times, then solid row 3 times. Work repeats as many times as desired to make a bigger shawl.

Ruffles

Row 1: Ch 4, [dc, ch 1] twice in same st, [ch 1, dc in next st] in each st to marker, [dc, ch 1] 5 times in marked st, *[dc in next st, ch 1], rep from * to last st, [dc, ch 1, dc, ch 1, dc] in last st.

Row 2: Ch 2, dc in each st across. Fasten off.

Finishing

Weave in ends.

Wide Ripple Scarf

Designed by Marie Segares

This wide scarf uses an openwork ripple pattern, but is still warm because it is long enough for several wraps around your neck. For a cozy look, try felting the scarf in the washing machine.

MATERIALS LIST

YARN

Stitch Nation by Debbie Stoller Bamboo Ewe (55% viscose from bamboo, 45% wool; 177yds/162m per 3.5oz/100g ball) in color #5830 Periwinkle, 3 balls

HOOKS AND NOTIONS

Size US M/N-13 (9mm) crochet hook, or size needed to obtain gauge

Yarn needle

GAUGE

Ch 44 and follow patt = 11-1/2" wide (Check your gauge for best results and fit)

FINISHED MEASUREMENTS

5.5" wide x 85" long/ 14cm x 216cm

Special Abbreviations

Dc4tog (double crochet four stitches together): *Yo, insert hook into next st, yo and draw up a loop, yo and draw through 2 loops, Repeat from * 3 more times, yo and draw through all 5 loops.

Crocheting the Scarf

Width can be adjusted by adding or removing multiples of 22 chains. Although it may appear at first that the peaks don't line up evenly, continue with the pattern as written for best results.

Ch 308.

Row 1: Dc in 4th ch from hook (counts as first 2 dc), dc in next ch, ch 2, sk 2 ch, dc in each of next 2 ch, ch 2, sk 2 ch, 2 dc in next ch, ch 3, sk 1 ch, 2 dc in next ch, [ch 2, sk 2 ch, dc in each of next 2 ch] twice, *sk 3 ch, [dc in each of next 2 ch, ch 2, sk 2 ch] twice, 2 dc in next ch, ch 3, sk 1 ch, 2 dc in next ch, [ch 2, sk 2 ch, dc in each of next 2 ch] twice, rep from * to end.

Row 2: Turn. Ch 3 (counts as dc), 2 dc in next ch-2 sp, ch 2, 2 dc in next ch-2 sp, ch 2, (2 dc, ch 3, 2 dc) in next ch-3 sp, [ch 2, 2 dc in next ch-2 sp] twice, *[2 dc in next ch-2 sp, ch 2] twice, (2 dc, ch 3, 2 dc) in next ch-3 sp, [ch 2, 2 dc in next ch-2 sp] twice, rep from * across. Finish with dc in top of turning ch.

Row 3: Turn, ch 3 (counts as dc), sk 3 dc, dc in each of next 8 sts (including ch and dc), 6 dc in ch-3 sp, dc in each of next 8 sts (including ch and dc), *dc4tog over next 4 dc, dc in each of next 8 sts (including ch and dc), 6 dc in ch-3 sp, dc in each of next 8 sts (including ch and dc), rep from * across. Finish with dc in top of turning ch.

Row 4: Turn, ch 3 (counts as dc), sk 3 dc, [dc in each of next 2 dc, ch 2, sk 2 dc] twice, 2 dc in next dc, ch 3, sk 1 dc, 2 dc in next dc, [ch 2, sk 2 dc, dc in each of next 2 dc] twice, *sk 4 dc, [dc in each of next 2 dc, ch 2, sk 2 dc] twice, 2 dc in next dc, ch 3, sk 1 dc, 2 dc in next dc, [ch 2, sk 2 dc, dc in each of next 2 dc] twice, rep from * across. Finish with dc to top of turning ch.

Rows 5-7: Repeat Rows 2-4.

Row 8: Repeat Row 2.

Row 9: Turn, ch 1, sc in each st across, working 6 sc in each ch-3 space. Fasten off.

Row 10: With sl st, join yarn to unworked loops of foundation ch at Row 1. Ch 1, sc in each st across. Fasten off.

Finishing
Weave in ends.

Fallen Leaves Shawlette

Designed by Anastasia Popova

This crescent-shaped shawl could be worn in few different ways - wrap it around your neck like a scarf or drape it over your shoulders. It's a simple shawl that is worked in one piece, from one point to another. The leaves edging is worked as you go.

MATERIALS LIST

YARN

500yds fingering weight yarn Sample shown in Patons Kroy Sock FX (75% washable wool, 25% nylon; 166yds/152m per 1.75oz/50g ball) in color #57012 Camo Colors, 3 skeins

HOOKS AND NOTIONS

Size US F/5 hook (3.75mm), or size needed to obtain gauge
Stitch marker
Yarn needle

GAUGE

21 stitches and 10 rows = 5" (13cm) in double crochet, blocked

FINISHED MEASUREMENTS

10.5" wide x 65" long/ 27cm x 165cm

Special Abbreviations

Cl (cluster): Work 3 dc together (yo, insert hook in specified st, draw up a loop, yo and pull through 2 loops on hook] 3 times, yo and pull through all loops on hook) in specified st.

Beg cl (beginning cluster): Ch 2, [yo, insert hook in cl of previous row, draw up a loop, yo and pull through 2 loop on hook] twice, yo and pull through all loops on hook.

Crocheting the Shawlette

Increase Section
Ch 9.

Row 1: 2 dc in 4th ch from hook (3 skipped ch count as dc), ch 2, skip next ch, dc in next 2 ch, ch 1, skip next ch, cl in last ch , turn (9 sts).

Row 2: Beg cl, ch 1, skip next ch, 2 dc in next dc, dc in next dc, ch 1, skip next 2 ch, 3 dc in next dc, ch 1, skip next dc, 3 dc in last st, turn (13 sts).

Row 3: Ch 3 (counts as dc), 2 dc in next st, dc in next dc, ch 1, skip next ch, dc in next dc, 2 dc in next dc, dc in next dc, ch 1, skip next ch 1, dc in next dc, 2 dc in next dc, dc in each dc to ch 1, ch 1, skip next ch, cl in last st, turn 16 sts).

Row 4: Beg cl, ch 1, skip next ch, dc in each st to 2 sts before next ch, 2 dc in next st, dc in next dc, ch 1, skip next ch, dc in next 4 dc, ch 1, skip next ch, dc in next 4 dc, turn (17 sts).

Row 5: Ch 3, dc2tog, dc in next dc, ch 1, skip next ch, dc in next dc, dc2tog, dc in next dc, ch 2, skip next ch, dc in next dc, 2 dc in next dc, dc in each dc to ch 1, ch 1, skip next ch, cl in last st, turn (17 sts).

Row 6: Beg cl, ch 1, skip next ch, dc in each st to 2 sts before next ch, 2 dc in next st, dc in next dc, ch 4, skip next 2 ch, dc3tog, ch 1, skip next ch, dc3tog, turn (16 sts).

Row 7: Ch 2, dc2tog (inserting hook in ch-1 sp and dc3tog), ch 2, skip next 2 ch, 3 dc in next ch, ch 2, skip next ch, dc in dc, 2 dc in next dc, dc in each dc to ch 1, ch 1, skip next ch, cl in last st, turn (19 sts).

Row 8: Beg cl, ch 1, skip next ch, dc in each st to 2 sts before next ch, 2 dc in next st, dc in next dc, ch 1, skip next 2 ch, 3 dc in next dc, ch 1, skip next dc, 3 dc in next dc, turn (13 sts).
Repeat Rows 3-8 four more times (43 sts).

Main Section

Row 1: Ch 3, 2 dc in next st, dc in next dc, ch 1, skip next ch, dc in next dc, 2 dc in next dc, dc in next dc, ch 1, skip next ch, dc in each dc to ch 1, ch 1, skip next ch, cl in last st, turn (45 sts).

Row 2: Beg cl, ch 1, skip next ch, dc in each dc to next ch, ch 1, skip next ch, dc in next 4 dc, ch 1, skip next ch, dc in next 4 dc, turn.

Row 3: Ch 3, dc2tog, dc in next dc, ch 1, skip next ch, dc in next dc, dc2tog, dc in next dc, ch 2, skip next ch, dc in each dc to ch 1, ch 1, skip next ch, cl in last st, turn.

Row 4: Beg cl, ch 1, skip next ch, dc in each dc to next ch, ch 4, skip next 2 ch, dc3tog, ch 1, skip next ch, dc3tog, turn.

Row 5: Ch 2, dc2tog (inserting hook in ch-1 sp and dc3tog), ch 2, skip next 2 ch, 3 dc in next ch, ch 2, skip next ch, dc in each dc to ch 1, ch 1, skip next ch, cl in last st, turn.

Row 6: Beg cl, ch 1, skip next ch, dc in each dc to next ch, ch 1, skip next 2 ch, 3 dc in next dc, ch 1, skip next dc, 3 dc in next dc, turn.

Repeat Rows 1-6 nine more times, then Rows 1-2 one more time (45 sts).

Decrease Section

Row 1: Ch 3, dc2tog, dc in next dc, ch 1, skip next ch, dc in next dc, dc2tog, dc in next dc, ch 2, skip next ch, dc in next st, dc2tog, dc in each dc to ch 1, ch 1, skip next ch, cl in last st, turn (43 sts).

Row 2: Beg cl, ch 1, skip next ch, dc in each dc to 3 sts before next ch, dc2tog, dc in next dc, ch 4, skip next 2 ch, dc3tog, ch 1, skip next ch, dc3tog, turn (41 sts).

Row 3: Ch 2, dc2tog (inserting hook in ch-1 sp and dc3tog), ch 2, skip next 2 ch, 3 dc in next ch, ch 2, skip next ch, dc in dc, dc2tog, dc in each dc to ch 1, ch 1, skip next ch, cl in last st, turn (41 sts).

Row 4: Beg cl, ch 1, skip next ch, dc in each st to 3 sts before next ch, dc2tog, dc in next dc, ch 1, skip next 2 ch, 3 dc in next dc, ch 1, skip next dc, 3 dc in next dc, turn (39 sts).

Row 5: Ch 3, 2 dc in next st, dc in next dc, ch 1, skip next ch, dc in next dc, 2 dc in next dc, dc in next dc, ch 1, skip next ch, dc in next dc, dc2tog, dc in each dc to ch 1, ch 1, skip next ch, cl in last st, turn (40 sts).

Row 6: Beg cl, ch 1, skip next ch, dc in each st to 3 sts before next ch, dc2tog, dc in next dc, ch 1, skip next ch, dc in next 4 dc, ch 1, skip next ch, dc in next 4 dc, turn (39 sts).

Repeat Rows 1-6 four more times (15 sts).

Next row: Ch 3, dc2tog, dc in next dc, ch 1, skip next ch, dc in next dc, dc2tog, dc in next dc, ch 2, skip next ch, dc in next st, dc2tog, ch 1, skip next ch, cl in last st, turn (13 sts).

Next row: Beg cl, ch 1, skip next ch, dc in next 2 sts, ch 2, skip next 2 ch, dc3tog, ch 1, skip next ch, dc3tog, turn (9 sts).

Next row: Ch 1, dc2tog (inserting hook in ch-1 sp and dc3tog). Fasten off.

Finishing
Weave in ends. Block.

Flower Shawlette

Designed by Anastasia Popova

This Flower Shawlette is a versatile piece. Made with cotton blend yarn, it's perfect for summer and spring. Try making it in beautiful wool or alpaca for a head-turning piece in the winter. The body of the shawlette and flowers are worked at the same time. Suggestions are given to make the shawlette longer and wider (and will affect the amount of yarn required).

MATERIALS LIST

YARN

450yds light worsted weight yarn. Sample shown in Jo-Ann Sensations Caribbean (56% cotton, 38% acrylic, 6% polyester; 465 yds/425m per 6 oz/ 170 g ball) in color #14 metallic turquoise; 1 ball

HOOKS AND NOTIONS

Size US G/6 (4.25mm) crochet hook, or size needed to obtain gauge
Stitch marker
Yarn needle

GAUGE

18 stitches and 8 rows = 4" (10cm) in dc, blocked

FINISHED MEASUREMENTS

11" wide x 72" long/ 28cm x 183cm

Special Abbreviations

Cl (cluster): Yo, insert hook in specified st and draw a loop, yo and pull through 2 loops] twice, yo and pull through all loops on hook.

Flower

Row 1: Ch 8, sl st in 6th ch from hook, ch 2.
Row 2: Ch 2, ([cl in ch-8 loop, ch 3] 5 times, cl) in ch-5 sp, sc in ch-5 sp 4 rows below to attach flower to the shawl (6 cl).
Row 3: Ch 1, [[sc, ch 2, cl, ch 2, sc) in next ch-3 sp] 5 times, sl st in next ch-2 sp, ch 2 (5 petals).

Crocheting the Shawlette

Increase Section

Row 1: Ch 6 (counts as dc, ch 1), in the last ch from hook work (dc, ch 1, dc), turn (5 sts).
Row 2: Ch 3 (counts as dc), dc in next ch-1 sp, ch 1, skip next dc, (dc, ch 1, dc) in ch-6 sp, turn (6 sts).

Row 3: Work Row 1 of flower, dc in first dc, [dc in next ch-1 sp, ch 1, skip next dc] across to last st, dc in last st, turn [6 sts (shawl) + 10 ch (flower)].
Row 4: Ch 3, [dc in next ch-1 sp, ch 1, skip next dc] across to last dc, (dc, ch 1, dc) in last dc, work Row 2 of flower, turn (8 sts + 6 cls).
Row 5: Work Row 3 of flower, 2 dc in next dc, dc in each st across, turn (9 sts + 5 petals).
Row 6: Ch 3, [dc in next dc, ch 1, skip next dc] to last 2 sts, dc in next dc, ch 1, dc in last dc, turn (10 sts).
Row 7: Ch 5 (counts as dc, ch 2), [dc in next ch-1 sp, ch 1, skip next dc] across, dc in last st, turn (12 sts).
Row 8: Ch 3, [dc in next ch-1 sp, ch 1, skip next dc] across, (dc, ch 1, dc) in ch-5 sp, turn (12 sts).
Row 9: Work Row 1 of flower, 2 dc in first dc, dc in each st across, turn (13 sts + 10 ch).
Row 10: Ch 3, [dc in next dc, ch 1, skip next dc] to last 2 sts, dc in next dc, ch 1, dc in last dc, work Row 2 of flower, turn (14 sts + 6 cl).

Row 11: Work Row 3 of flower, dc in first dc, ch 1, [dc in next ch-1 sp, ch 1, skip next dc] across to last st, dc in last st, turn (15 sts + 5 petals).

Row 12: Ch 3, [dc in next ch-1 sp, ch 1, skip next dc] across to last 2 sts, dc in next ch-1 sp, ch 1, dc in last dc, turn (16 sts).

Row 13: Ch 5, dc in each st across, turn (19 sts).

Row 14: Ch 3, dc in next dc, [ch 1, skip next dc, dc in next dc] to ch-5 sp, ch 1, dc in ch-5 sp, turn (18 sts).

Repeat Rows 3-14 two more times (40 sts). To make shawlette wider, work more repeats.

Straight Section

Row 1: Work Row 1 of flower, dc in first dc, [dc in next ch-1 sp, ch 1, skip next dc] across to last st, dc in last st, turn (40 sts + 10 ch).

Row 2: Ch 3, [dc in next ch-1 sp, ch 1, skip next dc] across to last dc, dc in last dc, work Row 2 of flower, turn (40 sts + 6 cl).

Row 3: Work Row 3 of flower, dc in each st across, turn (40 sts + 5 petals).

Row 4: Ch 3, [dc in next dc, ch 1, skip next dc] to last st, dc in last dc, turn (40 sts).

Row 5: Ch 5, [dc in next ch-1 sp, ch 1, skip next dc] across, dc in last st, turn (40 sts).

Row 6: Ch 3, [dc in next ch-1 sp, ch 1, skip next dc] across, dc in ch-5 sp, turn (40 sts).

Row 7: Work Row 1 of flower, dc in each st across, turn (40 sts + 10 ch).

Row 8: Ch 3, [dc in next dc, ch 1, skip next dc] to last st, dc in last dc, work Row 2 of flower, turn (40 sts + 6 cl).

Row 9: Work Row 3 of flower, dc in first dc, [dc in next ch-1 sp, ch 1, skip next dc] across to last st, dc in last st, turn (40 sts + 5 petals).

Row 10: Ch 3, [dc in next ch-1 sp, ch 1, skip next dc] across to last st, dc in last st, turn (40 sts).

Row 11: Ch 5, dc in each st across, turn (40 sts).

Row 12: Ch 3, [dc in next dc, ch 1, skip next dc] to ch-5 sp, dc in ch-5 sp, turn (40 sts).

Repeat Rows 1-12 four more times, then Rows 1-2 one more time. To make shawlette longer, work more repeats.

Decrease Section

Row 1: Work Row 3 of flower, dc2tog, dc in each st across, turn (39 sts + 5 petals).

Row 2: Ch 3, [dc in next dc, ch 1, skip next dc] to last 2 sts, dc2tog, turn (38 sts).

Row 3: Ch 5, dc in next ch-1 sp, skip next dc, [dc in next ch-1 sp, ch 1, skip next dc] across, dc in last st, turn (37 sts).

Row 4: Ch 3, [dc in next ch-1 sp, ch 1, skip next dc] to last 2 dc, dc in ch-5 sp, turn (36 sts).

Row 5: Work Row 1 of flower, dc2tog, dc in each st across, turn (35 sts + 10 ch).

Row 6: Ch 3, [dc in next dc, ch 1, skip next dc] to last 2 sts, dc2tog, work Row 2 of flower, turn (34 sts + 6 cl).

Row 7: Work Row 3 of flower, dc2tog, ch 1, [dc in next ch-1 sp, ch 1, skip next dc] across to last st, dc in last st, turn (33 sts + 5 petals).

Row 8: Ch 3, [dc in next ch-1 sp, ch 1, skip next dc] across to last 2 sts, dc2tog, turn (32 sts).

Row 9: Ch 5, skip first st, dc2tog, dc in each st across, turn (31 sts).

Row 10: Ch 3, [dc in next dc, ch 1, skip next dc] to dc2tog, dc2tog (inserting hook into next st and ch-5 sp), turn (30 sts).

Row 11: Work Row 1 of flower, dc2tog, [ch 1, skip next dc, dc in next ch-1 sp,] across to last st, dc in last st, turn (29 sts + 10 ch).

Row 12: Ch 3, [dc in next ch-1 sp, ch 1, skip next dc] across to last 2 sts, dc2tog, work Row 2 of flower, turn (28 sts + 6 cl).

Repeat Rows 1-12 two more times (4 sts + 6 cl).

Next row: Work Row 3 of flower, ch 2, dc2tog (inserting hook into next st and last st) (3 sts + 5 petals).

Do not fasten off.

Finishing
Work row of single crochet evenly along the straight edge, making 2 single crochet in each row.

Fasten off, weave in ends.

General Crochet Information

CROCHET HOOK CONVERSIONS

U.S. size	diameter (mm)
B/1	2.25
C/2	2.75
D/3	3.25
E/4	3.5
F/5	3.75
G/6	4
7	4.5
H/8	5
I/9	5.5
J/10	6
K/10·	6.5
L/11	8
M/13, N/13	9
N/15, P/15	10
P/Q	15
Q	16
S	19

Abbreviations

approx - approximately
beg - beginning
blo - back loop only
ch - chain
dc - double crochet
dc2tog - double crochet 2 together
hdc - half double crochet
pm - place marker
rem - remain(ing)
rep - repeat
rnd(s) - round(s)
sc - single crochet
sc2tog - single crochet 2 together
sl st - slip stitch
st(s) - stitch(es)
tog - together
TW - turn work

Stitches Used in This Book

If you are a U.K. crocheter, please note the U.K. conversions for some of the U.S. crochet terms used in the book.

U.S. crochet term	U.K. crochet term
chain (ch)	chain (ch)
slip stitch (sl st)	single crochet (sc)
single crochet (sc)	double crochet (dc)
half double crochet (hdc)	half treble (htr)
double crochet (dc)	treble (tr)
popcorn stitch	popcorn stitch
running stitch	running stitch
whip stitch	whip stitch

	LACE (0)	SUPER FINE (1)	FINE (2)	LIGHT (3)	MEDIUM (4)	BULKY (5)	SUPER BULKY (6)
WEIGHT	fingering, 10-count crochet thread	sock, fingering, 2ply, 3ply	sport, baby, 4ply	light worsted, DK	worsted, afghan, aran	chunky, craft, rug	super-chunky, bulky, roving
CROCHET GAUGE RANGE*	32–42 sts	21–32 sts	16–20 sts	12–17 sts	11–14 sts	8–11 sts	5–9 sts
RECOMMENDED HOOK RANGE**	Steel*** 6, 7, 8 Regular hook B/1 (1.4mm–2.25mm)	B/1 to E/4 (2.25mm–3.5mm)	E/4 to 7 (3.5mm–4.5mm)	7 to I/9 (4.5mm–5.5mm)	I/9 to K/10· (5.5mm–6.5mm)	K/10· to M/13 (6.5mm–9mm)	M/13 and larger (9mm and larger)

Yarn Weight Guidelines

Since the names given to different weights of yarn can vary widely depending on the country of origin or the yarn manufacturer's preference, the Craft Yarn Council of America has put together a standard yarn weight system to impose a bit of order on the sometimes unruly yarn labels. Look for a picture of a skein of yarn with a number 0–6 on most kinds of yarn to figure out its "official" weight. The information in the chart above is taken from www.yarnstandards.com.

Notes: * Gauge (what U.K. crocheters call "tension") is measured over 4" (10cm) in single crochet (except for Lace [0], which is worked in double crochet).
** US hook sizes are given first, with UK equivalents in parentheses.
*** Steel crochet hooks are sized differently from regular hooks—the higher the number, the smaller the hook, which is the reverse of regular hook sizing.